DESERTS

MICHAEL GEORGE

CREATIVE EDITIONS

Designed by Rita Marshall
with the help of Thomas Lawton

Published in 1993 by Creative Editions
123 South Broad Street
Mankato, Minnesota 56001

Creative Editions is an imprint of
Creative Education, Inc. This title is
published as a joint effort between
Creative Education, Inc. and American
Education Publishing.

Photo research by Kathleen Reidy

Photography by Animals Animals,
Tom Bean, Willard Clay, Comstock,
E. R. Degginger, Jeff Foott,
Les Manevitz, Masterfile,
Photo Researchers, Jay Simon,
and Harald Sund

Library of Congress
Cataloging-in-Publication Data

George, Michael, 1964–
Deserts / by Michael George.
Summary: Discusses the characteristics of
deserts and
the life they support.
ISBN 1-56846-054-6
1. Deserts—Juvenile literature.
[1. Deserts.] 1. Title.   91-503
GB612.G46 1991
508.315'4—dc20

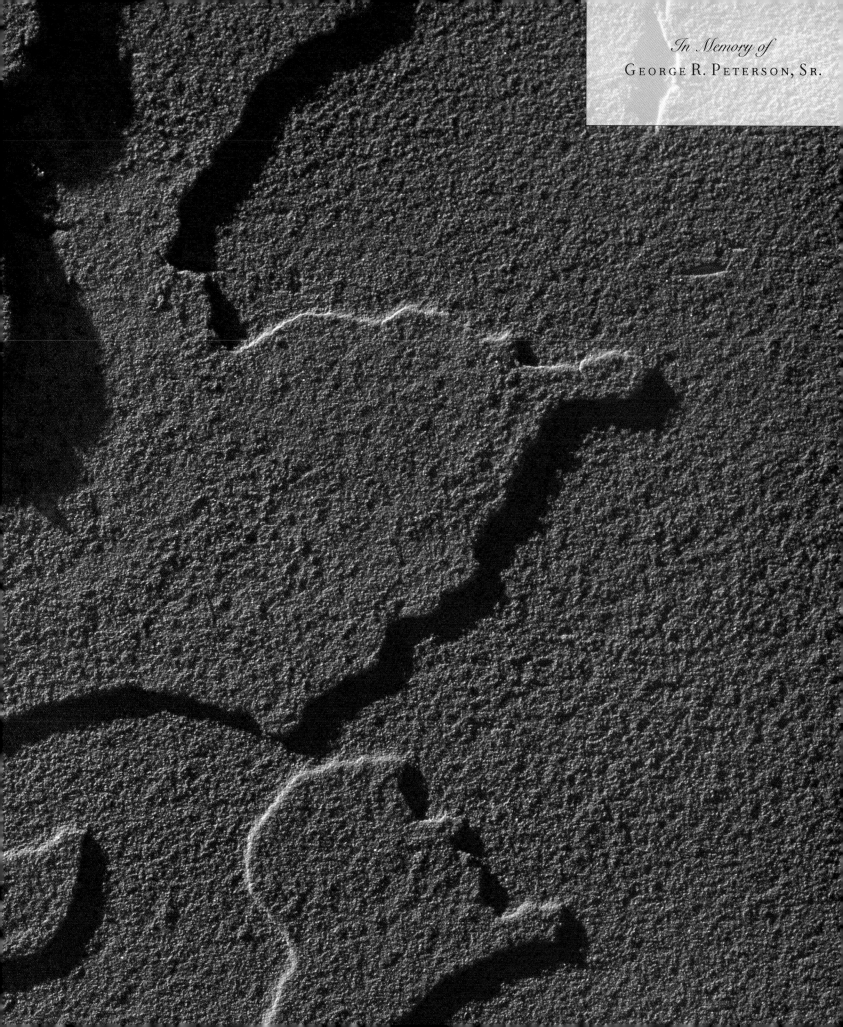

6

The word "desert" makes many people think of shriveled cacti, sun-scorched sand dunes, and shimmering waves of heat. They assume that the desert is a lifeless, waterless wasteland, baked by the Sun and battered by the wind. Yet despite its barren appearance, the desert is a fascinating place filled with unusual beauty. It is decorated with spectacular landscapes and is inhabited by an amazing variety of plants and animals.

The desert.

Deserts are areas that receive, on average, less than ten inches of rain per year. However, the amount of rainfall in a desert may vary greatly from month to month and from year to year. In fact, deserts often go without a single drop of rain for ten or twenty years. When it finally does rain, it pours. Ten inches of rain can fall from the skies within only a few hours.

A rare desert rainstorm.

9

Deserts cover about 20 percent of the Earth's land surface (an area about the size of Africa). The largest desert, the *Sahara* in northern Africa, is almost as large as the continent of Europe. The *Great Australian Desert* is the second largest desert in the world. It covers about half of the continent of Australia. Other major deserts include the *Arabian Desert* and the *Gobi Desert*, both located in Asia. Smaller deserts extend down the western coasts of North and South America.

The *Arctic Tundra* also qualifies as a desert, based on annual rainfall. On average, this region receives less than ten inches of precipitation each year, usually in the form of ice and snow. However, besides a lack of moisture, most deserts also have extremely high temperatures. Since the temperature rarely rises above freezing in the Arctic, this region is not a typical desert.

Tundra vegetation.

Most deserts are notoriously hot because of their lack of rain and other forms of moisture. In humid regions, clouds and water vapor prevent much of the Sun's energy from reaching the ground. But in dry, cloudless deserts, there is very little moisture to block the Sun's rays. As a result, air temperatures commonly reach 110 degrees Fahrenheit, and occasionally soar as high as 125 degrees—and that is in the shade! The ground gets even hotter than the air; with little to shield it from the Sun's rays, the desert floor can reach a temperature of 175 degrees.

Heat distortion of light.
Inset: A plant struggles to survive.

Although the desert can be scorching during the day, it can be downright cold at night. After the Sun sinks below the horizon, air temperatures can fall as much as 80 degrees, to a chilly 40 or 50 degrees Fahrenheit. In the Sahara Desert, the temperature once fell from a midday high of 126 degrees, to a nighttime low of 26.

Deserts have low nighttime temperatures for the same reason that they have high daytime temperatures. In humid areas, moisture and clouds not only prevent the Sun's energy from reaching the ground during the day, but also prevent heat from escaping at night. In the desert, there are no clouds or moisture to trap the warm daytime air. As a result, temperatures plummet as soon as the Sun goes down.

A harsh environment.

In addition to their extreme temperatures, deserts are also known for their unusual landscapes. The features most often associated with deserts are vast stretches of sand, called *Dunes*. The wind blows these seas of sand into small ripples and larger ridges. Sand dunes can grow up to eight hundred feet tall. Since the speed and direction of the wind are always changing, sand dunes continuously change size, shape, and even location.

Although many people assume that deserts are entirely blanketed by windblown sand, sand actually covers only about 15 percent of most deserts. The rest of the desert surface has been blown bare of loose sand and is covered by gravel, boulders, and various types of soil. Most desert soils contain abundant supplies of salts and minerals, but are too dry to support extensive vegetation.

Sand dunes.

Some types of desert plants do not bother trying to wring water from the dry soil. Instead, they tap pools of water that lie hidden beneath the ground. For example, the *Mesquite Tree* has roots that plunge forty feet beneath the desert floor. Still other types of desert plants store water in their leaves, roots, or stems. The barrel cactus, for instance, swells with water after it rains and slowly shrivels during times of drought.

Barrel cactus.

Perhaps the most original method of gathering water is that of the *Welwitschia*, found in the Sahara Desert. This unusual plant has long, gnarled leaves that collect morning dew. The dew drips off the leaves, soaks into the ground, and is absorbed by the Welwitschia's roots.

Besides having resourceful methods of obtaining water, desert plants also have ways to protect the valuable water that they collect. Since water evaporates quickly from leaves, many desert plants have tiny leaves. Other desert plants shed their leaves during dry periods. Plants also protect their valuable supplies of water with waterproof skins that limit evaporation, and spines that deter thirsty animals.

Welwitschia plant.
Inset: Welwitschia cones.

While most desert plants have ways to survive extended periods of drought, some do not even try. These plants may lie for years as dormant seeds buried in the desert soil. They spring to life only after a heavy rainfall. The individual plants live only a few short weeks before they shrivel beneath the dazzling desert sun. But before they die, the plants scatter seeds that will spring to life during the next rainy season.

Life can be brief in the desert.

Animals, like plants, also have resourceful techniques for surviving in the desert. Many desert animals obtain moisture from morning dew or from the foods that they eat. Other animals have more inventive methods for quenching their thirsts. The best-known desert animal, the *Camel*, actually stores water for later use. A camel can drink thirty gallons of water—nearly the amount needed to fill a bathtub—at one time. After drinking its fill, a camel can survive for a week or more without another drink of water.

Camels.

Perhaps the most fascinating method of obtaining water is that of the *Sand Roach*, found throughout the deserts of the southwestern United States. This remarkable insect actually absorbs water from the seemingly dry desert air. Its unusual method of "drinking" is so efficient that a sand roach can live its entire life without a sip of water.

In order to survive in the desert, animals must overcome hardships besides the lack of water. The desert's extreme temperatures are another threat to life. Few creatures can survive temperatures that are consistently higher than 100 degrees Fahrenheit. Therefore, animals try to avoid the desert floor during the day, when the temperature can soar over 150 degrees.

An owl rests inside a cactus.

37

One way to escape the extreme heat on the desert surface is to burrow beneath the ground. The temperature drops abruptly only a few inches below the desert surface. The *Kangaroo Rat* is one of the many desert animals that spends its days underground; like most burrowing animals, it comes above ground only after sunset. These animals feed and drink at night, when temperatures are cooler. As a result, the desert seems almost lifeless during the day, but comes alive with foraging spiders, insects, and rodents at night.

Desert temperatures drop sharply after sunset.
Inset: A burrowing tortoise.

Other animals escape the desert's midday heat by elevating themselves. Some types of snakes, for instance, climb into small shrubs during the day. Suspended just a few feet above the desert sand, the snakes stay significantly cooler and have a much better chance of survival. The camel also takes advantage of the relatively cool temperatures above the desert floor. Growing up to seven feet tall, camels stand where the temperature can be 50 degrees cooler than on the ground. Birds have the most effective method for escaping the hot desert surface. Hawks, eagles, and vultures soar high above the ground, where temperatures can be a comfortable 60 degrees Fahrenheit even on the hottest days.

Turkey vultures in the trees.

A *Desert* is a region of extreme drought, torrential floods, scorching heat, and bone-chilling cold. Yet despite these uninviting conditions, a desert is not a barren wasteland. Instead, it is a region decorated by exotic landscapes and inhabited by a variety of living things. A desert has a strange beauty that is found nowhere else on Earth.

Desert flowers.